100 Ways
To Make
$100

Financial Freedom

Justin C. LaCour

Copyright © 2018 Justin LaCour.

All rights reserved. No part of this book may be reproduced, stored, or transmitted by any means—whether auditory, graphic, photocopying, recording, mechanical, or electronic—without the written permission of both publisher and author, except in the case of brief excerpts used in critical articles and reviews. Unauthorized reproduction of any part of this work is illegal and is punishable by law.

*I dedicate this book to my wife and kids.
Thank you for the love and support...*

Contents

Introduction 9
1. Online Surveys 11
2. Pecan Season 13
3. Stocks 15
4. Dividends 17
5. Audiobooks 19
6. E-Books 20
7. Hard Copy Books 21
8. Ghostwriter 22
9. Essay Writer 23
10. Capstone Writer 24
11. Barbershop Owner 25
12. Flipping Cars 26
13. Flipping Houses 27
14. Flipping Jordans 28
15. Audiobook Producer 29
16. Author 30
17. Swim Instructor 32
18. Lifeguard 33
19. Certified Sex Coach 34
20. Firearm Instructor 35
21. Yoga Instructor 36
22. Valet 37
23. Website Designer 38
24. Guitar Teacher 39
25. Organist 40
26. Barber 41
27. Hair Braider 42

28. Piano Teacher 43
29. Slot Machines 44
30. Automobile Mechanic 45
31. Bellhop 46
32. Mobile Detailing 47
33. Landscaping 48
34. Focus Groups 49
35. eBay 51
36. Amazon FBA 53
37. Cryptocurrency 56
38. Day Care Center 57
39. YouTube Channel 58
40. Affiliate Marketing 60
41. Private Consulting 61
42. Metal Detector Professional 62
43. Aluminum Recycling 63
44. Pallet Recycling 64
45. Copper Recycling 65
46. Glass Recycling 66
47. Bonds 67
48. Peer-to-Peer Lending 68
49. Vending Machines 69
50. Online Vending Machines 70
51. Ginseng 71
52. Babysitting 72
53. Dog Walker 73
54. Uber/Lift Driver 74
55. Private Tutoring 75
56. Teak Wood Furniture 76
57. Referee 77
58. Housekeeping 78
59. Lemonade Stand 79
60. Student Instructor 80
61. Window Washing 81
62. Waiter 82
63. Store Delivery Services 83
64. Pizza Delivery 84

65. Dishwasher	85
66. Janitor	86
67. Sweet Potatoes	87
68. Caddy	88
69. Professional Photographer	89
70. DJ	90
71. Dog Trainer	91
72. Fantasy Football	92
73. Recycle Cell Phones	93
74. Dropshipping	94
75. Painter	95
76. Roofer	96
77. Sheetrock Removal	97
78. Scuba Instructor	98
79. Songwriter	99
80. Guitar Trainer	100
81. Website Developer	101
82. Private Moving Company	102
83. Apple Trees	103
84. Orange Trees	104
85. Fig Trees	105
86. Pear Trees	106
87. Selling CDs	107
88. Beats Creator	108
89. Paint & Wine Party	109
90. Art Sales	110
91. Business Consultant	111
92. Rent Party	112
93. Bingo	113
94. Car Wash	114
95. Catering	115
96. Bake Sale	116
97. Hot Dog Stand	117
98. Ice Cream Truck/Cart	118
99. Warehouse Worker	119
100. T-shirts	120
Conclusion	121

Introduction

THERE ARE HUNDREDS of ways to increase your cash flow. This book serves as a guide to get you started on your journey to financial freedom. None of the opportunities listed here are guaranteed but if you are motivated and persistent, you will surprise yourself with your level of success.

Online Surveys

THE FIRST WAY to make $100 is to complete online surveys. This is a legitimate way to make additional income. I would not quit my full-time job and rely solely on on-line surveys to pay all of your expenses. You can earn an additional $200 to $300 a month working online completing surveys part-time. I would complete surveys anytime and anywhere. If I was waiting at the barbershop to get a haircut, I'm not wasting time on Facebook and Instagram, I'm actually on my cell phone completing online surveys that the company sends you once you sign up. They have a lot of surveys that you can complete on your mobile device, including tablets. By the time, it was time for me to get my haircut, I had completed enough online surveys to pay for my haircut and the tip. Now, that is impressive. I love online surveys because there is no limit to your earning potential. People ask me all the time, how much can you make completing online surveys and I reply, it depends on how much money you want to make and how much time that you are going to dedicate to completing the surveys. When I'm watching football, basketball, or anything on television, I'm completing surveys at the same time. If everyone spent half of the time that they dedicate to social media, they would be surprised at how much money that they could earn completing online surveys. Time is money and it should be used wisely. If I'm out in town or going for a ride in my car, I'm thinking that I could be completing surveys now and earning money instead of wasting time. It is a good feeling to see multiple deposits to your bank account from different survey companies. Every time that I visit home, I always bring a couple of online survey checks with me to show my siblings to motivate them and to show them that this is real and that they can do this too. All you need is a computer, smartphone, or tablet and a high- speed internet connection and you can begin today. When you first get started in the online survey business, you will get the lower priced surveys but as you complete more and more surveys, they eventually get higher and higher. I remember completing a $25 survey in 5 minutes. It all depends on the particular survey and company that you are working with at the time. I hope that I have motivated you to get started today because I have been doing this since 2013 and it is always nice to have extra income to help support your family.

Pecan Season

THE SECOND WAY to make a quick $100 is to wait until pecan season starts in the fall and jump right in. Back in the day, you would have to get on your hands and knees to pick pecans, now there are tools that you can buy from your local hardware store so that you don't have to break your back bending over. Trust me, this is one investment that you will not regret. How do I know all of this? I have actually done it down south in Louisiana. I would wake up around 5:00 a.m. with my nephews and we would jump in the truck with our 50-pound bags and head to the pecan fields. You can make a lot of money doing this, depending on the location where you will be working. Make sure that it is your own property, a public park, or somewhere that is legal to pick pecans because you do not want any legal problems. On our first day out my nephews and I made $150 in an hour. The only reason that we stopped picking pecans that day is because the pecan exchange location was closing soon and we wanted to cash in before they closed but we had found a hot spot and I did not want to leave. If we would have stayed and cashed in the following day, we would have easily made at least $500 minimum one day. The next day, the word had spread to the rest of my family and when I woke up at 5:00 a.m. there were seven people waiting for me to go to work. They all had heard about how much money we made in an hour and they wanted to be a part of the team. So we all jumped in the truck and set out to make our fortune for the day. This day was a little more difficult because we had to go to several locations to fill our 50-pound bags. After four days of hard work, we made over $400 net profit. Who knew that you could make this amount of money just by picking pecans in your spare time? I was actually doing all of this work while I was on vacation. One of my cousins asked his mom why I was working on my vacation, and she could not give him an answer. When I heard of the conversation, I smiled and grinned because everything that I do has a lesson behind it, and I hope that he got the message.

Stocks

THE THIRD WAY to make $100 is to invest in the stock market. We are currently in a Bull Market and a lot of investors are stashing away cash and waiting on the next Bear Market. A lot of stocks are blowing up and this is scaring a lot of more experienced investors because if you listen to the Oracle of Omaha, Mr. Warren Buffett, he always says, "be fearful when others are greedy and be greedy when others are fearful." What this means is to do not invest in a stock when it up 200% in six months. It may be wiser to wait until there is a dip and the stock has a significant drop in the price per share and then you can buy your shares in the company. It is also important to remember that you are investing in the company and not in the individual stock. For example, I own a share of stock in Coca-Cola, that has been around for over 100 years but the stock price is less than $50 per share. Just because the price per share is low does not mean that the Coca-Cola Company is not profitable. So if you are going to get into the stock market, you should take an Accounting course so that you can read income statements and balance sheets for the different companies. Another great resource to get you started in the stock market is YouTube. I have learned tons of information on the stock market by watching YouTube videos in my spare time. Make sure to check out all of Warren Buffett's investing YouTube videos and it will help you get started on the right foot. Another great resource on investing is Benjamin Graham's The Intelligent Investor book. It will give you the foundation that you will need to be successful in the stock market and it will also help you to control your emotions when it comes to investing your money in the unpredictable marketplace. You will also be required to pay taxes on capital gains. It is 15% if you are in a 25% or higher tax bracket and 5% if you are in the 15% or lower tax bracket. The profits held from stocks held for less than a year are taxed at your regular income tax rate. All dividends earned on your stock holdings are taxed at regular income tax rates, not at capital gains rates. According to time.com/money, "if you sell stocks at a loss and those losses outweigh any gains you've made, the difference can be subtracted on your tax return, and used to reduce other income, like wages, up to $3,000 or $1500 for married couples filing separately." Time.com/money also states that, "if your losses are greater than that yearly limit, you can carry over the unused part to the next year and treat it as a loss you incurred in that next year." Remember this is general information on stocks and you should always consult with a tax expert when filing your income taxes.

Dividends

THE FOURTH WAY to make $100 is to buy dividend stocks. Not all companies pay a dividend, so you will have to do your homework when selecting a stock to invest in. Remember, if the offer is too good to be true, don't waste your time. It will only end one way and you will get discouraged. Some companies pay their dividend monthly and others pay it quarterly, it all depends on the company. For example, if a company is offering a share of their stock for $3.00 with a 15% dividend, you may want to take a thorough look at the company's balance sheet and income statement. If you don't know how to read a balance sheet and income statement, you need to start with the basics and take an accounting course and watch multiple YouTube videos on the stock market. You will be surprised at how much you can learn from watching YouTube videos. Actually, when I was in college, a lot of the classroom curriculum was YouTube videos and I was shocked because I was paying $750 a class and I was watching YouTube videos as part of the class curriculum. We are living in interesting times and the information is there, all you have to do is take advantage of the opportunities in front of you. There are hundreds of companies that pay dividend stocks. You should never buy a dividend stock just because it pays dividends. You need to do your homework and review the individual company's annual report, balance sheets, and income statements. This is why it is so important to invest in a college accounting course so that you are able to read a balance sheet and income statement. Some companies, such as Warren Buffett's Berkshire Hathaway company does not pay dividends because the company believes that they can do a better job with reinvesting the company's earnings than the individual shareholders. Some companies pay huge dividends over 10%, but this does not automatically mean that this is a good company. It may be a terrible company and by having a high dividend payout quarterly, they are able to attract investors with little to no experience in the stock market.

Audiobooks

THE FIFTH WAY to make $100 is to produce audiobooks on amazon.com. There are several steps before you get to the audiobook on www.acx.com, which is owned by Amazon. The easiest way to get started is to write an e-book and hardcopy book first, then you will be able to convert that same book to an audiobook with the help of one of the ACX producers. You have the option of paying the producer a flat rate for producing your book in their personal studio or you can use the 50/50 royalty share with the producer. This means that you will have to share all of your profits with the producer for as long as the book sells on Amazon, audible, and iTunes.

E-Books

THE SIXTH WAY to make $100 is to write your own e-books on kindle direct publishing through amazon.com. YouTube videos will help you throughout your journey. There are two options to receive royalties with your eBook. One is 35% and the other is 70% and it has a set price range for your eBook in each category. I highly recommend that you sell your first book for $0.99 because you are new to the market and you want to get reviews and establish reviews and rankings. Once you are established, you can always go back to your dashboard on kdp.com and change the price of your book. This is just advice and you can list your book at whatever price that you feel that it is worth. I hope that you will take my advice because it will help you in the long run. If you get lost at any time, please utilize YouTube and there is a step-by-step video on how to complete the entire process. Every book that you write can potentially generate you three separate forms of income. The first form of income is the e-book on www.kdp.com, the second form is a hardcopy book on www.createspace.com, and the third way is to convert the same book to an audiobook through www.acx.com. Some of the popular topics today in nonfiction books are relationships and finances. A great resource to see what type of books are selling is to check amazon.com for the best-selling books and the list is right in front of you. There is no need to reinvent the wheel, please use the resources that are available to you and you will thank yourself when you complete your first book and then you're hooked.

Hard Copy Books

THE SEVENTH WAY to make $100 is to write your own hard copy paperback book. This is the more traditional way to sell your personal book. Once your book is complete, you can sell it on www.createspace.com which is owned by Amazon. You will also have to get your personal book registered with www.copyright.gov so that your work can not be duplicated and sold under someone else's name. The interesting part about this process is that once your copyright is approved, you may receive offers in the mail from private publishing companies that are interested in publishing your book. The only drawback here is the fact that you are not allowed to publish or sell your book anywhere but through Amazon, because it is part of the process when you publish your book with them and they assign your book an International Standard Book Number.

Ghostwriter

THE EIGHTH WAY to make $100 is to ghostwrite books on www.fiverr.com. There are hundreds of people on Fiverr right now who are earning extra income by ghostwriting books for people who want their own book but do not enjoy or are not skilled at writing. You will be required to pay a one-time fee and all of the rights to your book will be legally owned by you. Your book will also have to be formatted in pdf format, epub or mobi so that you will be able to upload it to Amazon for publishing and you can also hire another freelancer on fiverr.com to accomplish this task for you for a small fee. The freelancer that I currently work with lives in the Philippines and he charges an affordable rate. You may have to work with a few freelancers before you find the one that is right for you and your individual needs.

Essay Writer

THE NINTH WAY to make $100 is to write essays online for anyone who requires your services. There are actually websites that support this new trending job. You will be required to write an essay for review to work on the website to ensure that you have a quality product. This job appeals more to people who love to write and want to use their natural talent to earn extra income on the side.

Capstone Writer

THE TENTH WAY to make $100 is to assist college students with their Capstone assignment. When I was in college and writing my Capstone, I could not get help from anyone to help me finish the assignment. I would have paid anything to have someone to help me to complete the project. I did not want someone to write the paper for me but I needed an assistant or mentor to help push me through the process. Anything is easier when you have someone on your team to support you!

Barbershop Owner

THE ELEVENTH WAY to make $100 is to buy your own barbershop. The best thing about being a barbershop owner is the fact that you can charge booth rent to all of the barbers that are working in your shop. You will be required to pay the expenses for the shop, so this should be added to your monthly budget plan to ensure that you are on track to financial peace.

Flipping Cars

THE TWELFTH WAY to make $100 is to flip used cars. I started flipping cars back in 2012. I thought that I was ready but I had no idea what I was doing. I purchased a used car for $6000 and that was the beginning of the end. I tried to get the car inspected by a mechanic before I purchased it, but the owner of the used car dealership assured me that the car was in good condition and if anything happened to the car within the first 90 days he would have me bring it in and have it fixed at the used car mechanic shop, which was attached to the used car dealership. This should have set off a lot of alarms in my head but I was focused on flipping cars and ignored all of the signs of a bad deal. Just like clockwork, the car began to give me problems in the first week after purchase. I called the Used Car Dealership Owner and explained to him that the car needed servicing and he said that he could repair it at a discounted rate at his repair facility. So it is good to do your homework first and have any car that you plan on buying checked out by a certified mechanic before spending your hard earned money. I finally was able to flip the used car at a loss of $6000. I had spent $1000 in repairs plus the purchase price of $6000 which placed me $7000 in the hole. There are some great deals out there, you just have to be careful and if the dealer will not let you get the car checked out by a certified mechanic that you pick, please move on to a different dealership to avoid the heartache that I had to go through on my first used vehicle purchase.

Flipping Houses

THE THIRTEENTH WAY to make $100 is to flip houses. There are a lot of shows that flip houses such as Flip or Flop, etc. You can watch these shows for six months but you will not become an expert on real estate by watching shows on television. So I would highly recommend that you earn your real estate license and this will give you a solid foundation to flip houses and to actually learn the basics of the real estate industry.

Flipping Jordans

THE FOURTEENTH WAY to make $100 is to flip Jordans online. A lot of barbershops do this already due to the fact that it is an easy sell. I currently live in Japan and guess what the Japanese barber has for sale in his barbershop. You are right, he has three different types of Jordans for sale in a display case. So this is an international selling opportunity that anyone can take advantage of. I have personally sold Jordans on eBay and I usually dropship the product from another company for profit or I will buy the product and store the inventory in my home office. The last pair of Jordans that I sold was right before Christmas of last year and I opened the product to ensure that it was not damaged. Once I saw the shoes, I didn't want to ship it to the customer who had already paid me via PayPal but I did not want to disappoint a customer that was looking forward to getting a new pair of Jordans for Christmas. So as you can see this can be very profitable if you have the time and drive to take advantage of this unique opportunity.

Audiobook Producer

THE FIFTEENTH WAY to make $100 is to produce audiobooks for www.acx.com which is owned by Amazon. This opportunity does require a studio because when you produce audiobooks for authors through acx.com, there is a quality assurance check through the website and if it is not a high-quality product, it will get rejected and sent back to the producer and author for corrections and will not be accepted until it meets acx.com standards. So if you own a studio already and you are looking for another form of income, this a golden opportunity for you to create income that lasts for years. They are two ways to get paid. The first one is to charge the author a flat rate for recording their book with no more payments and the second way is a 50/50 royalty share that will get paid as long as the book is selling on acx.com and iTunes. The producer gets $50 of a $100 royalty share and the author gets the other half and this is automatically managed by acx.com so you will not have to worry about the author sending your payments on time.

Author

THE SIXTEENTH WAY to make $100 is to write your own books. I know that this may be intimidating to some of you but anyone can write a book but it takes a dedicated person to create a quality product. Everyone says that they want to write a book in the future but very few people actually follow through and finish the product. I was one of those people. I always say that I was going to write my own book after I retired from the military but when I got stationed in Japan on my last tour of duty, I decided to start writing and publishing my books on amazon.com. Once you write, publish, copyright, etc. your first book, it starts to snowball and you are hooked after your first couple of online sales. I was really excited when I received my first European payment and it motivated me to keep writing. This is not a get rich quick scheme, it takes hard work and dedication to write a book and you will never get started if you continue to procrastinate. So, the easiest way to get started is to start watching YouTube videos and start writing. People ask me all the time, how did you learn how to publish books on Amazon and my response to that question is by watching YouTube videos. You will be surprised at how much educational content is on YouTube. When I was going to college to complete my Bachelor's degree, a lot of the course material was YouTube videos. This was shocking to me because I was paying around $750 a class to complete my degree and a lot of the content was YouTube videos and some of the teachers were promoting their own personal books that they had personally written as part of the course curriculum which is obviously a violation of the institution's ethics' policy. As a side note, do not take your online reviews personal. Please use the reviews as constructive criticism and this will help you to focus on your next project. So the only thing holding you back is you. Please don't worry about being the next Steven King, just get your first book published and it will motivate you to write and publish your second book.

Swim Instructor

THE SEVENTEENTH WAY to make $100 is to work part-time as a swim instructor. You will be surprised at how many military bases hire swim instructors for the military dependent children on bases all over the world. So it really does not matter where you live because there are military bases all over the world who are in need of qualified swim instructors. Also, the city and private swimming pools in your city hire swim instructors to help with their busy summers.

Lifeguard

THE EIGHTEENTH WAY to make $100 is to apply for a part-time job as a lifeguard. There are a lot of places in town that hire lifeguards during the summer. Some examples are private pools, public pools, military bases, beaches, etc. This a seasonal job but it is worth the easy money and at the same time you are getting a tan while at work.

Certified Sex Coach

THE NINETEENTH WAY to make $100 is to get qualified as a Certified Sex Coach. This may be new to a lot of people but this is an actual certification in the New Sexual Revolution. Of course, you will have to be mature enough to professionally complete the certification and actually make any money from potential clients.

Firearm Instructor

THE TWENTIETH WAY to make $100 is to apply for a job as a Firearm Instructor. This is a good part-time job for a Police Officer, Military personnel, etc. This can be a very rewarding job, especially on military and civilian gun training facilities across the country.

Yoga Instructor

THE TWENTY-FIRST WAY to make $100 is to apply for a job as a Yoga Instructor. This job is not only lucrative in the civilian world but also on military installations stateside and overseas. I am in Japan and there are Yoga Instructors that teach yoga classes every week on base and all of the military dependents and servicemembers attend the class every week.

Valet

THE TWENTY-SECOND WAY to make $100 is to valet park vehicles at a club, restaurant, etc. This is one job where you can make a lot of money in one night from a couple of generous people. Some of the best days to work as a valet are Valentine's Day, holidays, etc.

Website Designer

THE TWENTY-THIRD WAY to make $100 is to design websites. A low-end designer can earn around $40 an hour. While the high-end designers charge anywhere from $75 to $100 an hour. The average price is around $59 an hour for an average website designer. So the higher your skill level, the more money that you can potentially earn.

Guitar Teacher

THE TWENTY-FOURTH WAY to earn $100 is to conduct guitar lessons in-home or in-studio. I would highly caution against the in-home lessons due to safety concerns. This is an easy way to earn cash by passing on your skills that you have acquired over the years to potential clients. You can utilize social media to help with advertising your business until you can get your own website developed.

Organist

THE TWENTY-FIFTH WAY to earn $100 is to offer organ lessons for local or online private lessons. The organ is a difficult instrument to master and by studying the pedal technique, this could make the process a lot easier. The primary difference between an organ and a piano is the foot pedals. It takes a long time to master the organ, so this could earn you a lot of money in your spare time.

Barber

THE TWENTY-SIXTH WAY to make $100 is to earn money as a licensed barber. This can be a lucrative job if the barber is the best in town. For example, I am in Japan and the best barber in town is right across the street from the Air Force Base. He charges around $15 and the local nationals, American civilians and contractors, Navy, Air Force, Marines, and Army servicemembers go to this one Japanese barber every day to get a haircut. I have been here for over three years and I get a haircut every week and I pay the barber $20 on each appointment. That is $80 a month from one customer and he only takes about 15 minutes to cut my hair. The barber works nine hours a day, appointments are every 30 minutes, and so that is eighteen customers a day. Eighteen times fifteen equals $270 a day not including tips. The shop is open for six days a week which comes to $1620. The monthly total for one barber is $6480 not including tips. As you can see, you can earn a lot of money as a barber once you acquire the best skills in town.

Hair Braider

THE TWENTY-SEVENTH WAY to earn $100 is to braid hair. This is a unique skill set because everyone is not good at braiding hair. In Japan, you can earn a substantial amount of money by braiding hair because of the military bases in the area. Most people braid hair at their personal houses because they do not own their own hair salons. The hair salons on base and out in town do not know how to braid hair because of the cultural differences. This presents a great opportunity for the Americans in the area that are experts at braiding hair. There are a lot of opportunities to make extra income and sometimes you have to think outside of the box and you'll be surprised on how many options that are available to you.

Piano Teacher

THE TWENTY-EIGHTH WAY to earn $100 is to conduct piano lessons at your home or in-studio. This a good way to keep your skills polished and earn some extra cash in return. The average cost of a piano lesson is from $15 to $40 depending on your location and the skill level of the teacher.

Slot Machines

THE TWENTY-NINTH WAY to make $100 is to visit your local casino and play the slot machines. This is not something that you want to do on a regular basis because the house always wins. I won $150 on my birthday and tried to go back the following day and lost most of it. You can get lucky if you play in moderation and you have to know when to quit. I remember playing at a casino in Washington State and one of the women there hit the jackpot on the slot machine for $18,000. She was screaming and yelling for one of the staff members to cash her out and escort her to the cashier in the casino. At the same time, she told her friend who was sitting next to her to save her seat at the slot machine because she was coming back to play again. The lady then cashed in her $18,000 jackpot and started playing the same slot machine ten minutes later. Some people do not know when to quit and eventually lose everything in the process. So if you can control yourself and quit while you are ahead, you can potentially make a lot of money playing the slot machines.

30

Automobile Mechanic

THE THIRTIETH WAY to make $100 is to work as a shadetree or certified mechanic. First of all, I will explain the definition of a shadetree mechanic. A shadetree mechanic is a person that works on cars at their own home or garage and charges a fair price to customers that cannot afford to take their used vehicles to the dealership for professional repairs. A mechanic can make a lucrative salary especially if the person is a certified Mercedes Benz or BMW mechanic. The dealerships only hire the best of the best because they have to maintain their reputation and if the car repairs are mediocre, the dealership will be required to repair or replace the vehicle with one of the same value.

Bellhop

THE THIRTY-FIRST WAY to make $100 is to work as a bellhop. A bellhop is a person that helps patrons with their luggage while checking in and out of hotels. If the bellhop is working at the Waldorf Astoria in New York, he or she can make a lot of money on tips from wealthy patrons who frequent the luxury hotel. This is another option to build wealth on your journey to become debt free.

Mobile Detailing

THE THIRTY-SECOND WAY to make $100 is to create your own mobile detailing business. There is an American here in Japan that has built his own mobile detailing business across the street from the Air Force Base. He gets business from the local nationals and from the Navy, Army, Air Force, Marine Corps servicemen and women. There are opportunities everywhere and it is up to you to make the first step and use your gift to make you a lot of money.

Landscaping

THE THIRTY-THIRD WAY to make $100 is to start your own landscaping business. Some people are real good at landscaping and this may start off as one or two yards and then those customers may refer you to someone else and it starts to snowball at that point. For example, the summer after I graduated from the ninth grade, I decided to work as a landscaper for the summer so that I can earn enough money to purchase tennis shoes for my tenth grade school year. So I worked the whole summer and right before I was leaving to go to the shopping mall, another customer approached me and asked for my business card. So once you get started and build a reputation at a fair price, your business will gain momentum and you can become very wealthy.

Focus Groups

THE THIRTY-FOURTH WAY to generate extra income is through focus groups. This is one of my favorites because at the end of the focus group, the manager hands you a $100 bill and sometimes a $100 check. When I first heard about people getting $100 to attend a 2 hour focus group, I was skeptical like most people. When I showed up to the office, there was a secretary at the front desk and she took my information and had me sit in the waiting area where there was lunch on standby. I was surprised to see other people there already with Harry Potter books, movies, and memorabilia. The focus group was on Harry Potter and they were prepared for the focus group questions. The hardest part in regards to being selected for a focus group is the initial questioning over the phone. This is where you will find out if you are eligible for the focus group. I remember being screened out for a $225 focus group because of the initial questions that the company asked you when they are filling their quotas. The other side of that is that if they call you in for a focus group, you will get paid at the end of the meeting in cash or check. How many of you have been to a police station? Ok, then you are familiar with the interview room. When you are in a focus group, there are observers behind a double-sided mirror that can see you and they record and watch everything during the focus group. If you do not participate much during the focus group, they will call you out and ask you if you have any input or opinion on the topic or particular question. They have to pay you once you leave, so they want to make sure that they get their money's worth. I also remember conducting a focus group on Haagen-Dazs ice cream container. They went into great detail in regards to the container design in relation to customer appeal and how the particular product made you feel. You will be amazed at the depth of the various focus groups. Once you complete your one or two-hour focus group, you and your fellow group members will line up and head towards the front desk where the secretary is waiting with the $100 bill or check. I was shocked to receive $100 for two hours of questioning. I always thought that opportunities like this were fiction and that the media was making all of this up to get attention until I actually did it myself. Now, focus groups pay a lot more than surveys but they are not easy to screen and get approved for. So, if you get the opportunity to participate in a focus group and you have the time, please take advantage of this unique opportunity because it pays to give your opinion.

eBay

THE THIRTY-FIFTH WAY to make $100 is one of the older ways to make income which is through eBay. I have been a member of eBay since 2012 and I was surprised to see that I have generated over $6000 in sales and I only remember selling about $2000 worth of merchandise. That is the sweet thing about making passive income, you are making money in your sleep. Even though Amazon is killing it right now, eBay still has millions of customers and sellers every day. So it is ok to have an Amazon and eBay account. It depends on how motivated you are and how much money you want to make. I first realized my skill when I was in the fifth grade and my teacher sent me to the principal's office for selling pencils in class for profit. She told the principal that she had told me to stop selling pencils in class. I explained to the principal that this was the first time that I was told about this and I also explained to the principal that I was an A Honor Roll student and why would I create a distraction or problem in the classroom. He agreed with me and sent me back to class. It is hard for some people to get started because everyone does not have what it takes to be an entrepreneur. It may take longer than 8 hours a day, especially when you are first starting your own business. You have to be motivated and dedicated to putting in the time and effort. Most people quit and go back to their 9-5 job. The only problem with that is the fact that most people dread going to their job every day. Until you step outside of your comfort zone, you will be stuck in the rat race. You can sell products from your personal storage on eBay or you can dropship the item from various suppliers in the United States and overseas. For example, I received an order the other day for a razor blade and I dropshipped the item from China. It takes longer to ship from overseas but as long as you list the shipping time in the description and the buyer purchases your product, you are good to go. I love eBay because they use PayPal and as soon as the customer purchased the razor blade I received an e-mail from PayPal of the deposit and an e-mail from eBay letting me know that the product was sold and that it was also available for relisting. I immediately added the shipping number to the listing so that the customer could track his order and relisted the razor blade on my account. The company allows you to list 50 new products a month (up to 200 total). I did not want to wait until the next month to list my new products, so I paid $0.30 for each additional product over 50 for the month. The fourth quarter of each year is the best time to sell on eBay due to the holidays, so roll up your sleeves and make it happen. The only thing holding you back is you. If you have negative people around you, you need to close your circle. My circle is very small for a reason. Who you choose to associate with says a lot about who you are as a person.

Amazon FBA

THE THIRTY-SIXTH WAY to create passive income is through Amazon FBA or fulfillment by Amazon. This is a great way to start your own private E-Commerce business. Amazon has over 300 million active customers in their system waiting to purchase new products with the click of a button. It is real easy to get signed up for Amazon FBA. I actually used YouTube to help me sign up for the business. It was not difficult and it guided me step by step. Once your account is created, you can list as an individual and Amazon will charge you $0.99 per purchase or you can take advantage of fulfillment by Amazon, which is highly recommended, to help support your business. This particular service is $39.99 a month. It may be hard when you first start but anything worthwhile is going to involve some sacrifice. If it were easy, everybody would be doing it. Once you are signed up, you need to list your first product. I recommend a product that is small, light, and inexpensive to ship. Most of the entrepreneurs outsource from overseas and the lighter the product, the cheaper the shipping costs. If you want to sell any kind of health or supplement products, I highly recommend going through the United States due to the Food and Drug Administration and various inspections that the product must past including customs before entering the United States. Amazon allows you to sell on Amazon.com, Amazon (Canada), and Amazon (Mexico). So, the potential to earn lots of money is unlimited. A god starting point to find a profitable product is to go to amazon.com and check the best sellers list. This will give you a good idea of the product or products that you would like to begin selling online. Once you get you product listed on Amazon FBA, you will need the shipping address of the manufacturer that you are using to enter into the system. This can be time-consuming, especially if your manufacturer is overseas. I remember e-mailing my first manufacturer in China and I asked for his shipping address and he replied, "Why do you need my shipping address?" His response told me three things right away. One, he was inexperienced in business, two, he was rude to a potential long-term customer, and three, I was going to look for another manufacturer. Once you get the shipping address from the manufacturer, you will need to enter it into your Amazon FBA account. Then you will continue to fill in your account information. You will have to label each of your products with a bar code so that Amazon can scan and store your products in the fulfillment warehouse. If you do not want to attach a bar code to each one of your products, you have the option to pay Amazon $0.20 per bar code to label the products for you. For example, if you have 100 products that you are sending to the fulfillment center, you will pay Amazon $20 to label all 100 products. When you are first starting out, it is a good idea to send the products to your house. This way you can inspect the quality of the products and print and label each product and save the $0.20 Amazon labeling fee. After you have inspected and labeled all of your products, you will need to print the UPS shipping label (cheapest), so that you can take your product to the U.S. Post Office and mail to the Amazon Fulfillment centers on the East and West Coast. The reason that you want to mail your product to both coasts is simple. If someone orders one of your products on Amazon.com from Florida, the Amazon Fulfillment center on the East Coast will ship the product to the customer and vice versa. Once your products are at the Amazon Fulfillment centers, all you have to do is ensure that your inventory is stocked. Once an order is placed, Amazon will pack, ship, and deliver the product to the customer. They also deal with returns and customer service. So, all you need to do is sit back and monitor the deposits directly to your personal bank account. Remember to keep your inventory stocked so that you do not miss out on potential sales.

Amazon has the one click pay system and your inventory can potentially be depleted in one week, so you will need to ship your products to the fulfillment centers in a timely manner. If you are shipping from China, it can take over a month to get your products to the fulfillment centers, so please keep that in mind as you are restocking your inventory.

Cryptocurrency

THE THIRTY-SEVENTH WAY to make $100 is to invest in cryptocurrency. The most popular type of cryptocurrency is Bitcoin. I currently own a percentage of Bitcoin, Bitcoin Cash, Litecoin, and Ethereum. The good thing about cryptocurrencies is the fact that you don't have to buy a whole coin to invest in the market. In the stock market, you have to buy the whole stock, you cannot invest in a percentage of a stock. A lot of people think that the cryptocurrency market is a waste of time and money but I'd rather have something invested in the market just in case the critics are wrong again. In December of 2017, Bitcoin market value was selling over $19,000 a coin. Everyone was losing their mind trying to get in on the action and all of a sudden, the price started to drop. It is currently July 2018 and Bitcoin is valued at $6,217.39. It has been holding steady around $6,000 for the last couple of months and this may be a good time to invest in the cryptocurrency due to the fact that it gained a lot of steam last year around the holidays. The easiest way to get started is to sign up for an account at www.coinbase.com. There are different sites that sell cryptocurrency but a lot of them are illegal. Always conduct research on anything that you are going to invest in. The new blockchain technology will change the way the world handles money and it is a good idea to understand the basics of this new technology so that you are not left in the dark in this new era.

Day Care Center

THE THIRTY-EIGHTH WAY to make $100 is to open your own day care center. For example, if you open up a daycare center in San Diego, Ca close to 32nd Street, you will be able to target the military dependent children. The average cost for day care for one child in San Diego is over $100 a week. If the child is a newborn it is going to cost more due to more care is required to take care of a newborn baby. Ensure that you have cameras installed everywhere to protect the kids and to protect yourself from lawsuits or false claims of abuse or neglect.

39

YouTube Channel

THE THIRTY-NINTH WAY to make $100 is by setting up your own YouTube channel. It is not hard to set up a YouTube channel and there are actual YouTube videos that will guide you step by step to help you set up your channel. There are additional videos to help you monetize your accounts so that you can get paid for your videos. You can also take advantage of AdSense, which places ads on your videos that are popular to help you generate income. One of the new changes with YouTube personal videos is the fact that you must have at least 1000 subscribers and 4000 hours of watch time before you can get paid. So the more popular your videos are, the more money you will make. You will get paid off of your video's views, watch time, and advertisements. If you go into your account, it will actually show you the different countries around the world that have viewed your video. I was surprised to see that my videos were being viewed in Afghanistan. So, you never know who will be interested in your video content, you just have to get started and promote your channel through social media, friends, and word of mouth. Remember the more videos that you upload, the more money that you will make. For example, if you have 1,000 videos uploaded and each video gets 100 views per day, which would generate you approximately $100 in passive income per day. That is good money considering the minimum wage in the United States is sad. Remember this is passive income, so this extra money that you are making without having to physically do anything once the video is edited and uploaded into the system. If you have real friends they will support you and watch your videos to help support you on your journey. If your friends and family will not take the time to watch a 5-minute video to help support and encourage you, you made need to close your circle. If I had a friend with a YouTube channel and I knew that they were trying to establish themselves in the business, I would play their video every chance that I got, but that's a real good friend.

Affiliate Marketing

THE FORTIETH WAY to make $100 is to make yourself marketable so that affiliate marketing companies search for you to advertise their products. Every year, companies spend billions of dollars on marketing their products online. For example, Kylie Jenner has millions of fans on Instagram, so affiliate marketing companies will contact her directly to ask if she would advertise their product and in return, she is paid royalties every time a product is advertised on her page. Some of the companies require that the customer actually clicks on the advertisement and buy the product or any product on their website within 24 hours (Amazon affiliate marketing), but all companies have their individual requirements that have to be met so that the person advertising the product can receive their royalty payments directly to their checking account. Keep in mind, companies are not going to contact you if you only have 100 friends that are following you, so the more popular you are on social media increases your earning potential.

Private Consulting

THE FORTY-FIRST WAY to make $100 is through private consulting. One of the most popular types of consulting is small private business consulting. This can be an easy source of income for someone with consulting skills in a specific industry. A friend of mines does private business consulting and she makes a lot of money in her spare time. She has a regular job and she works as a consultant in the evenings during the week and on weekends and holidays.

Metal Detector Professional

THE FORTY-SECOND WAY to make $100 is to invest in a metal detector. I have a friend that is a metal detector professional and he goes to the beach in Japan on the weekends to search for hidden treasures. You will be surprised at what you can find on a beach in Japan or the United States. Every day someone in the world loses their expensive jewelry and valuables while on vacation and they do not have time to search the entire resort before they fly back home. This is where the metal detector professionals come in and clean house. Some beaches ban metal detecting and you have to be aware of the local laws before you are arrested for using metal detectors illegally on private property.

Aluminum Recycling

THE FORTY-THIRD WAY to make $100 is to recycle the aluminum cans that you use every day. For example, there are over one billion servings of Coca-Cola served every day in more than 200 countries and if you could collect a small fraction of those aluminum cans, you can make a lot of money. I like recycling because it is good for the environment plus you get paid in cash for your hard work. You don't have to wait two weeks or a month to get paid, the money is paid out as soon as the employee at the recycling center writes you a ticket and you walk to the cashier to pay you per pound of aluminum sold. A lot of homeless people in the United States recycle cans so that they can make enough money to survive another day. There are also a lot of middle-class people recycling cans to make a little extra cash on the side, so jump right in and save the cans that you are throwing in the trash every day and you could potentially earn money from your hard work. This is also a good way to teach your kids how to earn money and not expect everything to be handed to them for doing nothing.

Pallet Recycling

THE FORTY-FOURTH WAY to make $100 is to recycle pallets. This is very interesting because I did not know that you could recycle pallets until I got a job at a warehouse and the customers started taking the pallets from the back of the building. As the customers were driving off with the pallets, I asked the manager why they were taking the pallets and he said that they recycle them for money at the recycling center which left me in shock because he was not trying to stop them from stealing the pallets. If they are worth money at the recycling center, I'm sure that the owner of the company would like to keep those pallets on the back of the building.

45

Copper Recycling

THE FORTY-FIFTH WAY to make $100 is to recycle copper in your spare time. The average price for scrap copper in the United States is over $2.00 lb. That is easy money if you have copper in your garage already. This is a huge problem in the United States because a lot of people search abandoned houses and building under construction and remove all of the copper piping so that they can sell it at their local recycling center. This is why you have to provide an identification when you exchange copper so that it can be accounted for with the local authorities. If you show up at the recycling center with 100 lbs. of copper piping, chances are the police have already notified all local recycling centers to be on the lookout for large quantities of copper piping trying to be exchanged and you will go straight to jail. So if you have scrap copper around your house that you personally own, take it to your local recycling center and turn it into cash in minutes.

Glass Recycling

THE FORTY-SIXTH WAY to make $100 is to recycle glass bottles. This is another easy way to earn money by collecting those empty beer bottles around your house and neighborhood. A lot of people are embarrassed to go around dumpsters to recycle glass bottles but homeless people recycle every day and this is how they buy food to survive for another day. I would be more embarrassed if I could not pay my bills because I was too proud to recycle bottles. Remember that you get paid by the pound, so the glass bottles pay a little more than plastic bottles because of their weight.

Bonds

THE FORTY-SEVENTH WAY to make $100 is to invest in government bonds. Bonds pay periodic interest payments and they also repay the face value on the maturity date. This is another option for those of you who are not fans of the stock market. The most current 30-year bond has an interest rate over 2%. This is not a significant amount of money when you factor in the annual inflation rate for the United States is over 2%.

Peer-to-Peer Lending

THE FORTY-EIGHTH WAY to make $100 is to invest in peer-to-peer lending. In peer-to-peer lending, you are operating as the bank and you are loaning customers micro-loans. The only problem with this is the fact that the person borrowing the money from you may not pay you back and you are stuck in a bad situation. Some of the popular peer-to-peer lending sites are Lending Club, Prosper, Funding Circle, etc. There is a required initial deposit with the sites to get started with the company. For example, there is a $1000 minimum initial deposit to get started and once your account is funded, there is a $25 minimum investment per note.

Vending Machines

THE FORTY-NINTH WAY to make $100 is to buy vending machines and get them strategically placed at stores in your neighborhood. My cousin has a vending machine in the front of his house because he got tired of broke people always asking for something to drink. This is a very lucrative business here in Japan with a can of Coca-Cola costing over $1. You can see how fast this could add up in just one day. The vending machines here is Japan have everything from sushi to beer to coffee and tea. You don't have to cook anything, all you need to do is go to a vending machine which is on every corner, including construction sites. One snickers bar costs $1.25 in the Japanese vending machine. Last month, that same snickers bar was $1.00 but people are still buying them every day.

50

Online Vending Machines

THE FIFTIETH WAY to make $100 is to invest in online vending machines. When most people think about vending machines, they think about the traditional vending machines that are outside of stores. The online vending machine is the wave of the future and the millennial generation is taking advantage of this new opportunity. You will have to create advertisements online to send customers or traffic to your online vending machine website. There is a 14-year-old girl on YouTube and she owns her own vending machine website and it generates her about $75 a week. That is not bad for a 14-year old that is working online in her spare time.

Ginseng

THE FIFTY-FIRST WAY to make $100 is to grow ginseng on your private property. Ginseng takes around seven years to grow and it is worth a lot of money. There is actually a television show that is dedicated to people selling ginseng in West Virginia. The plant grows all over the state and it grows in fertile forests. In West Virginia, ginseng grows wild in the moist forests of the state and poachers come from far and wide to cash in on the prized perennial herb. This is a million dollar crop and if you are not familiar with ginseng, you may want to do a little research because it can pay dividends in the future.

Babysitting

THE FIFTY-SECOND WAY to make $100 is to babysit for friends, family, and strangers. This is a profitable job if you have the credentials. You have to get qualified to babysit kids and this includes a CPR qualification. The time that you invest to get qualified to babysit kids will pay off in the long run. This is usually a job that teenagers take advantage of to earn money while in high school but anyone can take advantage of this opportunity to earn some extra cash.

Dog Walker

THE FIFTY-THIRD WAY to make $100 is to walk dogs. This is very popular in New York. Dog walkers can make a lot of money if you have the motivation to use social media to acquire new clients. There was a woman on the Dave Ramsey radio show that was making tons of money walking dogs in her spare time to pay off debt. There are unlimited amounts of ways to make money in your spare time but most people say that they want to make more money but they are not willing to do what it takes to bring them to the next level.

Uber/Lift Driver

THE FIFTY-FOURTH WAY to make $100 is to work as an Uber or Lift driver in your spare or full time. The only problem with this job is the fact that you will get paid on the year of car that you are driving. For example, if you are driving a 2018 Mercedes Benz, you will get paid more money than someone driving a 2000 Honda. You will also have to deal with drunk customers who may throw up in your back seat and you will have to clean your car and try to get another customer after the stench is out of the car. It may be a good idea to have a video camera in your car, due to the fact that a lot of customers have been allegedly assaulted by Lift and Uber drivers.

55

Private Tutoring

THE FIFTY-FIFTH WAY to make $100 is to use your natural skills in a certain subject or subjects to tutor students at a high school or college. I was always gifted in math and I never studied one day for a math class in high school or college. I used to tutor Geometry for free to one of my classmates in high school. She was having a hard time understanding the topic so I agreed to tutor her after school. I arrived at her house to tutor her and I was greeted by her boyfriend because he was uncomfortable with a male tutoring his girlfriend. I guess he figured that I was up to something because I was tutoring his girlfriend for free. The ironic thing about his story is the fact that the girl that I was tutoring had a boyfriend that was in college at the time but he was not able to help her in a high school topic that he had supposedly taken already. So you can make a substantial amount of money tutoring in your spare time. There is always someone who needs help in various topics and all you have to do is to make yourself available.

Teak Wood Furniture

THE FIFTY-SIXTH WAY to make $100 is to sale teak wood furniture. Teak wood is considered the gold standard for decay resistance. This is very popular in areas that have an abundance of precipitation. Seattle, WA would be a great place to invest in teak wood due to the amount of rain that the city receives on an annual basis. I lived in Everett, WA for four years and it rained at least nine months out of the year, so if you are going to buy outdoor furniture and you live in an area with a lot of annual precipitation, it would be wise of you to invest in teak wood.

Referee

THE FIFTY-SEVENTH WAY to make $100 is to work as a referee at a basketball, football, or soccer game. This is an easy way to earn some cash for the local elementary school basketball game or military baseball game. The military bases here in Japan are always looking for a good referee for the multiple sports events year round. This is another great way to increase your cash flow.

Housekeeping

THE FIFTY-EIGHTH WAY to make $100 is to clean houses in your neighborhood. You can earn money from lazy people who don't want to clean their own house. The military base in Japan has a cleaning service that charges over $100 to clean your house one time. So you can see how lucrative this business can be. The good thing about this business is the fact that you can clean more than one house in one day. I am usually able to clean my whole house from top to bottom in about two hours. So you can earn a lot of cash in one business day.

Lemonade Stand

THE FIFTY-NINTH WAY to make $100 is to start your own lemonade stand. This may be embarrassing for a grown man or woman to open a lemonade stand but it is more embarrassing to not be able to pay your bills. Every time that I see someone trying to help themselves in a private business venture, I always buy their products because I want to encourage them to keep moving forward. When I was growing up, there was an older lady in the neighborhood that sold ice pops and snicker bars. You may think that you cannot make a significant amount of money by selling these products but you will be surprised at how fast the sales add up and how fast the word spreads around the neighborhood. If you charge $1 for a cup of lemonade and you sell 100 cups of lemonade in one day you just made $100. If you sale lemonade every day for 30 days, you just made $3000 in one month. If you only get half the sales, that is still $1500 in one month selling lemonade. As you can see, your effort adds up fast when you don't make excuses and get the job done.

Student Instructor

THE SIXTIETH WAY to make $100 is to work as a student instructor. Student instructors earn enough money for a person looking for a part-time or full-time job. There are also incentives for veterans to work as ROTC instructors where you can retire in 10 years. This is a great opportunity for our veterans to have meaningful work after retiring from the military.

Window Washing

THE SIXTY-FIRST WAY to make $100 is to wash office building windows. This is a job that can get real busy when you get a contract with a huge commercial building with hundreds of windows. You will have to wear a safety harness when you are window washing high-rise buildings.

Waiter

THE SIXTY-SECOND WAY to make $100 is to work as a waiter in any of the hundreds of restaurants in the United States. The salary is not that high but you make up the difference in tips. I usually tip my waiter at least 20% every time that I go out to eat. So if everyone tipped their waiter at least 15% they would make at least $50 a night at any decent restaurant.

Store Delivery Services

THE SIXTY-THIRD WAY to make $100 is to apply for a job to deliver products for stores in your neighborhood. More and more stores are starting to offer this service and it is getting very popular in areas where the elderly have a hard time getting to and from the store. This is a great idea and you can earn some cash on the side if you have the drive to work a couple of extra hours every week.

Pizza Delivery

THE SIXTY-FOURTH WAY to make $100 is to deliver pizza full-time or part-time. I always tip the pizza delivery person at least 20% especially if they are delivering the pizza in the snow or 100 degrees fahrenheit temperatures. In Japan, the pizza delivery company has its own pizza delivery cars. You do not have to use your own car and that is great due to the wear and tear placed on your vehicle when delivering pizzas.

Dishwasher

THE SIXTY-FIFTH WAY to make $100 is to apply for a job as a dishwasher. This is hard work but it is another source of income. I remember washing dishes from 6:00 am to 6:00 pm while serving in the military. This was hard work and it really makes you appreciate everything that you have and it will make you a stronger person if you don't quit and give up. Most restaurants hire dishwashers to keep clean silverware, plates, pots, pans, etc. to keep their business operating without any delays. Can you imagine going to a restaurant and you have to wait for the owner to wash the dishes because the dishwasher did not show up for work or quit without notice? This may not be the most respectful job but a very important job in any restaurant.

Janitor

THE SIXTY-SIXTH WAY to make $100 is to work as a janitor. This may not be the most glamorous job but it pays the bills. I remember the janitor from my elementary school in the fourth grade. His son actually went to the same school and his son was embarrassed when his dad would walk by with the trash can or mop in his hand. This taught me a valuable lesson at a very young age. That valuable lesson was the fact that sometimes you have to swallow your pride to feed your family.

Sweet Potatoes

THE SIXTY-SEVENTH WAY to make $100 is to sell your own sweet potatoes. The sweet potatoes in Japan cost over $4.00 a pound. I was in shock to see how much they were charging for sweet potatoes. They are a lot cheaper at the farmer's market. A lot of local farmers in Japan sell vegetables on the side of the road at a discounted price. When I was growing up in Louisiana, there was a guy selling sweet potatoes out of the back of his truck and when he drove by our house he would yell, "potato man!" Most people would think twice about buying potatoes out of the back of a truck but it was real popular in Louisiana when I was growing up in the 1980s.

Caddy

THE SIXTY-EIGHTH WAY to make $100 is to work as a caddy. There is always a job open for a good caddy on the golf course. Tour caddies can earn salaries from $1,000 to $2,000 per week. Caddies make more than $100 for each 18-hole round, but the real pay comes from tips. The average salary is around $120 for carrying two bags 18 holes.

Professional Photographer

THE SIXTY-NINTH WAY to make $100 is to work as a professional photographer. My wife and I found a private photographer online while we were living in San Diego, Ca. She agreed to meet us at this beautiful building near the park and she took some professional pictures and I still have one of the photos as a screensaver on my cell phone. She only charged us $100 for the entire photo shoot. So if you are good at taking pictures and you own a professional camera, you may have a future in this industry.

70

DJ

THE SEVENTIETH WAY to make $100 is to work as a DJ. There are a lot of DJ jobs available online. Every time that we have an event on the military base, we hire a private DJ and they are paid by the hour. A good DJ can make around $200 to $300 for one night's work.

Dog Trainer

THE SEVENTY-FIRST WAY to make $100 is to work as a dog trainer. Dog trainers average around $7 to $29 an hour. The more experienced dog trainers earn over $100 per hour depending on the country. Some people have been training dogs their whole life and they have never used their gift for monetary gains.

Fantasy Football

THE SEVENTY-SECOND WAY to make $100 is to play fantasy football. This is a very popular gambling game in the United States. Unfortunately, it is not available in Japan. Some of the popular fantasy football sites are Draft Kings, FanDuel, etc. When I first started investigating the fantasy sports' sites, I discovered that it covers not only football but also baseball, basketball, etc. It is quick to earn money playing fantasy sports and it is also very easy to lose a lot of money. I remember playing fantasy football and I was so excited because I was winning a lot of money during the first game, but that does not mean anything because you have to wait until all the players that you have selected to be on your team have played for the day and then your money is tallied up and paid to your account. So it is a gamble to play fantasy sports and if you do not have the money to lose, I would not waste my time. The more experienced sports' fans seem to profit playing fantasy sports due to their infinite wisdom.

73

Recycle Cell Phones

THE SEVENTY-THIRD WAY to make $100 is to recycle cell phones. There are actually vending machines in shopping malls that collect old cell phones and it will disburse a dollar value depending on the type of phone that you are recycling. I have about 4 old cell phones that I need to sale when I get back to the United States. If your friends and family have old phones that they want to throw away, you can collect all of those phones and recycle them for cash. A lot of people do not know that their old phones are worth a lot of money and they are missing out on a golden opportunity.

Dropshipping

THE SEVENTY-FOURTH WAY to make $100 is by dropshipping products on amazon.com. The great thing about this strategy is the fact that you can use multiple sources as your supplier. I usually source from China but sometimes there is an issue with the supplier, so I always have two backup sources and sometimes I will have the product at my home office. You always want to have more than one supplier. This way if there is an issue with your main supplier, you have a backup and you will not lose your customer base. Once you run out of stock on Amazon (Amazon FBA), they will pull your product listing and it will show out of stock when you log into your account. So, you have to be proactive, because this is a legitimate business and you want your customers to receive their products promptly. So when your inventory is getting low, you should already be online or on the phone ordering more supplies to restock the Amazon Fulfillment Warehouse on the East and West Coast. At the same time, you are going to have to manage your finances. If you are not good at managing finances, I highly recommend that you hire an accountant. If you spend all of your money on frivolous things, you will not be able to restock your product and your product will be pulled from the product listing on Amazon and this could negatively affect your ranking on Amazon, which directly affects your sales revenue.

Painter

THE SEVENTY-FIFTH WAY to make $100 is to apply for odd jobs as a painter. I never painted a day in my life until I joined the U.S. Navy. I have been painting for years while serving my country. I have painted everything from bilges on ships to exhaust stacks on the exterior of the ship. There are always people on indeed.com looking for painting services. A real good painter can make a fortune painting part-time or full-time. Zip recruiter is currently hiring professional painters for $30,000 to $43,000 a year. You can also assist a professional painter to get your foot in the door and eventually start getting jobs on your own to maximize your income.

Roofer

THE SEVENTY-SIXTH WAY to make $100 is to work as a roofer. Roofers get paid a lot of money due to the hazards involved with working on the rooftop. You have to know what you are doing or you will not get paid. I worked as a roofer with zero experience. This was a recipe for disaster but we were helping the local community in Mississippi in the aftermath of Hurricane Katrina. The job is a lot easier if you have a nail gun. If you don't have one, you will be in for a world of hurt. The other important safety tip is to get a tetanus shot. One of my friends stepped on a nail while we were working on the roof and he had to be rushed to the emergency room. Also, make sure that you are wearing steel toe boots for your safety. It is a great idea to have at least one professional roofer on your team because you get what you pay for. When we finished the roofing job, all of the shingles were not even and the entire roof had to be fixed by a professional roofer.

Sheetrock Removal

THE SEVENTY-SEVENTH WAY to make $100 is to search for jobs for sheetrock removal services. I have removed sheetrock from houses in Mississippi after the Hurricane Katrina disaster. We were not paid a dime because we were tasked with helping the community as active duty servicemembers. So after work at 5:00 pm, I arrived at my second job at The Home Depot and there were customers from New York buying supplies in the millwork department. They told me that they were getting paid $10,000 to remove sheetrock from a single family home. I was in shock because I had helped three families remove sheetrock at that point and I had not received a penny. So there is a lot of money in the sheetrock removal business as long as you have someone to help you carry the sheetrock to the dumpster.

Scuba Instructor

THE SEVENTY-EIGHTH WAY to make $100 is to work as a scuba instructor. There are several scuba instructors here in Japan. Scuba instructors average around $35,000 to $40,000 a year in the United States. If you love the water and you are a certified dive instructor, you can make extra money in your spare time. This job is for professionals only because if you don't know what you are doing, you can potentially cause someone to drown because of your incompetence.

Songwriter

THE SEVENTY-NINTH WAY to make $100 is to write songs. Unfortunately, everyone does not have this talent but if you are one of the select few that do have this gift, you can earn a lot of money writing songs for artists. You may have heard of Kandi Burruss from Xscape (a popular female singing group in the 1990s). She actually writes songs for other artists and she gets paid a lot of money for her hard work and dedication to her craft. That is why she is living like royalty in Atlanta, Ga. If you are a great songwriter, you will have to step out of your comfort zone and advertise yourself on social media so that you can be rewarded for your hardwork. The only thing holding you back is fear of rejection.

Guitar Trainer

THE EIGHTIETH WAY to make $100 is to use your guitar skills to train young and older students who want to learn how to play the guitar. The average salary for a guitar trainer is around $40,898 per year. This is a unique skillset because there are not too many great guitar players that have the time to dedicate to training others. A lot of the professional guitar players are busy getting ready for their next show, so this provides a great opportunity to land a job or jobs as a guitar trainer.

Website Developer

THE EIGHTY-FIRST WAY to make $100 is to develop websites for the millions of potential customers on social media. The average salary for a website developer is around $66,130. The lowest-paid developers earn $35,390 and $119,550 on the high end. The internet is here to stay and anyone who specializes in computer software, website development, or information technology has a bright future. These are the people who will take the new blockchain technology to the next level and apply that knowledge to solve the problems of the future. Blockchain is a growing list of records that are linked using cryptography. Cryptography is defined as the art of writing or solving codes. Blockchain technology is at the core of the infamous bitcoin cryptocurrency.

Private Moving Company

THE EIGHTY-SECOND WAY to make $100 is to start your own private moving company. A lot of people do this already buy it is usually for friends and family. This can be a great family business if you have a huge family that does not mind a little hard work. My pregnant friend scheduled a moving company to come out to help her move because her husband was going on deployment with the military. So on the day that the moving company was supposed to start moving my friend to her new house, no one showed up. You can imagine how scary this could be for a pregnant female that is left alone by her spouse who is deployed by the military with no family in the area. So if you are going to be a legitimate moving company, you will have to be dependable because you can have a significant impact on someone's personal life. You will need your own moving truck but when you first start your business, you can always take advantage of the U-Haul company and their low rates until you can get established in the moving business.

Apple Trees

THE EIGHTY-THIRD WAY to make $100 is to grow your own apple trees in your backyard. This will take a while due to the fact that it takes 2 to 10 years for an apple tree to mature and produce fruit. Once the trees are bearing fruit, you can hand pick them and sell them on the side of the road or at your local farmer's market. In Japan, local farmers sell their fruit and vegetables every day on the side of the road and I always stop to buy fresh fruit to support the local community.

Orange Trees

THE EIGHTY-FOURTH WAY to make $100 is to grow orange trees in your backyard. An orange tree can produce fruit as early as 3 years. The tree may not have grown to its full height in 3 years but it will still produce fruit. You may want to grow this tree in a fenced in yard due to the fact that there are people who will steal your fruit and sell it on the same street that you live on. The price of fruit in grocery stores is ridiculous and there are thousands of people who would rather visit there local farmer's market before spending twice the amount in a grocery store.

Fig Trees

THE EIGHTY-FIFTH WAY to make $100 is to grow fig trees in your backyard. Fig trees bear fruit twice a year but the fruit is only edible once a year. I grew up in Louisiana with a fig tree in our backyard and we used to eat the figs off of the tree for years. Our tree was about twelve feet tall, so it was mind blowing to find out that some varieties of the fig trees can grow up to 50 feet tall. I've never purchased figs from the store but they are used in preserves and you can find these for sale online and in small stores throughout the country. Fig fruit is also used as a laxative and the leaf of the plant is used for diabetes, high cholesterol, and skin conditions such as eczema, psoriasis, and vitiligo.

Pear Trees

THE EIGHTY-SIXTH WAY to make $100 is to grow pear trees in your backyard. Pear trees mature and bear fruit in four to six years when it can blossom freely. Pear trees are very popular in the south and there are local farmers that sell fruit every day and most people will buy from a local farmer because of the freshness of the fruit and the cheap price compared to the local grocery store.

Selling CDs

THE EIGHTY-SEVENTH WAY to make $100 is to sell your own CDs. Every time that I would go to a restaurant in San Diego, there was someone outside selling CDs. I would buy CDs from the local entrepreneurs for around $5. Some of the music actually sounded good and some of it was mediocre. If you know how to create your own music CDs, you can sell them out of the trunk of your car. This is how a lot of artists in the music industry got started with their music careers. Nicki Minaj sold over $1,000,000 in mix tapes before she became the global star that she is today.

Beats Creator

THE EIGHTY-EIGHTH WAY to make $100 is to create your own beats. Back in 2013, one of my co-workers made $20,000 by creating beats in his spare time. I was surprised that you could make this type of money by working only part-time. I discovered that artists are always searching for new beats on the internet and if you don't give yourself a chance, you will never know how much money that you can earn. The more beat samples that you produce, the higher your chances are of getting offers from potential artists.

89

Paint & Wine Party

THE PAINT AND wine parties are becoming more and more popular in the United States. My wife and I had a paint and wine Anniversary party last year and it was a lot of fun and when we were finished we hung the pictures on the wall in our dining room area. This is trending right now and all you need to do is buy the paint, paint brushes, canvas, music, and wine. This is an easy way to earn money by hosting paint and wine parties.

Art Sales

THE NINETIETH WAY to make $100 is to sale your own art. If you have a very special art skill and you have a whole house of art that you have been accumulating, you can sell your art online on eBay, garage sale, or open your own shop. It's a good idea to try and sell your product online first to see if there is an audience for your hard work. Social media is also a great test platform for your new business. If my friend was trying to sell art online, I would buy at least ten pieces of art to support my friend and to encourage them to keep grinding.

Business Consultant

THE NINETY-FIRST WAY to make $100 is to work as a private business consultant. Consulting is a great way to work as your own boss and you will not have to worry about working a traditional job. Of course, you have to have knowledge and skills in the particular business that you will be consulting and you can utilize social media to help jumpstart your business.

Rent Party

THE NINETY-SECOND WAY to make $100 is to have a rent party. A rent party is where you have a regular party planned but you charge everyone at the door a set price. So they are paying to party with you and helping you pay your rent at the same time. The host usually provides the drinks and food since you are paying to attend their party and this can be done whenever you come up short on your rent money. I would not recommend trying to pull this off every month because this is going to get old real fast and people will not show up anymore.

93

Bingo

THE NINETY-THIRD WAY to make $100 is to play bingo. There is a bingo game every Wednesday and Sunday on the base in Japan and the payout is ridiculous. I was there one Sunday and this older man won $3000 with the automatic bingo machine and 30 minutes later his wife won another $3000 on her automatic bingo machine and they both got up and walked out of the bingo game $6000 richer in less than an hour. This was my first time playing bingo on base and I was in shock because they were giving away thousands of dollars for one single game of bingo. So as you can see, you can make a lot of money playing bingo in your local neighborhoods. The myth that old people are the only ones that play bingo is not true, a lot of young people play bingo every Wednesday and Sunday on base. The entry fee per game is around $30 and that gives you a shot at over $1000 per game, so the odds are on your side.

Car Wash

THE NINETY-FOURTH WAY to make $100 is to sponsor your own car wash. This is a great way to earn some extra cash. I used to wash cars with The Boys and Girls Club in Louisiana at the local Pizza Hut. We learned when you accept donations only, you earn a lot more money than setting a specific price. This one customer drove up to me and handed me a $100 bill and drove off. He did not even get his car washed but wanted to support and encourage us to work hard and you never know who is watching and willing to help. I have also gone to the local AutoZone and asked if I could hold a car wash in their parking lot and they said yes because we were drawing in customers for the store and buying our soap and Armor All from the company. They also allowed us to use their water free of charge. So if you don't mind rolling up your sleeves and getting a little dirty, you can easily make a $100 in less than a day. Remember donations only gets you paid a lot more money than charging $10 a car.

Catering

THE NINETY-FIFTH WAY to make $100 is to start your own catering service. My wife's aunt has her own catering service where she bakes cakes, cookies, etc. I did not know that you could make a substantial amount of money by having your own private catering business but she showed me that it is possible. Every year during Christmas time when she is baking cookies for her business, she sends us some holiday cookies. So if you have a cooking background and your friends and family are always telling you that you can open your own business, this may be very profitable for you and your family.

Bake Sale

THE NINETY-SIXTH WAY to make $100 is actually fun if you love to bake. I love to bake and I usually bake cookies or biscuits on the weekend. If you are good at baking, you can start off by giving away samples at work to see how your co-workers will respond. You can also hand out food on the streets to get feedback on your baked goods. I always buy products from the Girl Scouts or anyone that I see that is trying to hustle and make money by working hard and trying to earn an honest living. Sometimes I would not take the product but I still would give a donation for their efforts.

Hot Dog Stand

THE NINETY-SEVENTH WAY to make $100 is to start your own hot dog stand business. This is a great idea due to the fact that a ton of people eats hot dogs every day. If there was a hot dog stand outside of my house on the street, I would buy a hot dog every day after work as an appetizer prior to dinner. So you can imagine how many other people would be willing to buy a hot dog after work or right before going on a walk or walking their dog through the neighborhood. The inventory is cheap and can be sourced from Wal-Mart at a minimum cost. You may have to spend a little money on the stand or you can build your own stand and save that money also.

Ice Cream Truck/Cart

THE NINETY-EIGHTH WAY to make $100 is to invest in an ice cream truck or cart. The ice cream truck is very popular in every neighborhood in the United States. You can purchase the ice cream from Wal-Mart and you can buy the freezer for your truck from the Home Depot. The investment will pay off when you start charging a $2 for an ice cream bar and you purchased a box of eight bars for $5. That is $11 profit on each box of ice cream sold in one day. When I lived in San Diego, Ca there was an older male who would walk through the neighborhood with an ice cream cart with a little bell on it and every time that he walked by my apartment I would go outside and buy two ice cream cones. The next day would come by and I was buying the more ice cream cones along with my neighbors. I started to notice that the ice cream man was getting a lot of business and by the time he got to my apartment, the ice cream that I liked was sold out. You can make a lot of money selling ice cream, especially during the summertime. If you cannot afford a truck, I recommend buying or building an ice cream cart. The cart that the guy in my neighborhood used was a small refrigerator inside a small wood frame with wheels and an axle. So it was a simple build but it got the job done at minimum cost.

Warehouse Worker

THE NINETY-NINTH WAY to make $100 is to apply for a warehouse job. I worked in a warehouse for a Japanese man while I was in High School to earn some pocket change. I did everything from sweeping to painting and everything in between. There are jobs everywhere and if you really want to work, you will find something eventually.

T-shirts

THE ONE-HUNDREDTH WAY to make $100 is to sell your own t-shirts. First, you will need to come up with a logo and find a company that will produce your shirts at the lowest price. A lot of people source their shirts from the Philippines. The exchange rate for the Philippines is currently $1 US dollar to 53.47 Philippine Piso. So you will have a huge profit margin by selling those shirts in the United States. Social media is also a great resource to take advantage of and advertise your product online to your followers.

Conclusion

IN CONCLUSION, there are thousands of ways to make $100. We have just scratched the surface with the first one hundred. If you really want to earn more cash flow for you and your family, all you need to do is use your head to create positive cash flow and acquire assets. Once you acquire assets and receive more cash flow, buy more assets and you will eventually become wealthy as long as you minimize expenses and eliminate liabilities. Remember that finances are the #1 cause of divorce and relationship problems in the United States. All of the resources that I have shared with you are just sources of income. I am not guaranteeing anyone success by trying any of the 100 ways to make $100, but if you apply yourself and never give up, you will position yourself in the best place to become successful in whatever you decide to focus on. I hope that this helps you on your journey to financial freedom. Good luck!

www.ingramcontent.com/pod-product-compliance
Lightning Source LLC
Chambersburg PA
CBHW020437220526
45464CB00002B/747